BARACK OBAMA
PRESIDENT FOR CHANGE

Peter Hicks

WAYLAND

Wayland
338 Euston Road
London NW1 3BH

Wayland Australia
Level 17/207 Kent Street
Sydney, NSW 2000

Senior Editor: Camilla Lloyd
Designer: Rob Walster
Picture Researcher: Shelley Noronha

Acknowledgements: p. 23 My Inspiration
from p. 151 *Obama: The Historic Campaign in
Photographs* by Deborah Wills & Kevin Merida.

Picture acknowledgements: The author
and publisher would like to thank the
following for allowing their pictures
to be reproduced in this publication:
Cover: © Rex Features Ltd; © Obama For America/
Handout/Reuters/Corbis: 6, 7, 8; © Bagus
Indahono/epa/Corbis: 9; © Handout/Reuters/
Corbis: 10; © Rudy Sulgan/Corbis: 11; © Joe
Wrinn/Harvard University/Handout/Corbis: 14;
© Joe Wrinn/Harvard University/Handout/Brooks
Kraft/Corbis: 15; © Pete Souza/White House/
Handout/CNP/Corbis: 16; © Obama For America/
Handout/Reuters/Corbis: 18; © Ira Wyman/
Sygma/Corbis: 19; © Frank Polich/Reuters/
Corbis: 20; © Jason Reed/Reuters/Corbis: 21;
© Matthew Cavanaugh/ epa/Corbis: 22; © John
Zich/zrImages/Corbis: 24; © KeystoneUSA-ZUMA/
Rex Features: 26; © Anthony Behar/Sipa USA/Rex
Features: 27 © Jim Young/Reuters/Corbis: 28; ©
Getty Images: 5, 20, 25; © AFP/Getty Images: 12,
17; © Rex Features Ltd: 4, 13, 27, 29.

British Library Cataloguing in Publication Data:
Hicks, Peter, 1952-
Barack Obama. - (Inspirational lives)
1. Obama, Barack-Juvenile literature. 2.
Presidents-United States-Biography-Juvenile
literature. 3. African American politicians-
Biography-Juvenile literature.
I. Title II. Series
973.9'32'092-dc22

ISBN: 978 0 7502 6695 6

2 3 4 5 6 7 8 9 10 11

Printed in China

Wayland is a division of Hachette Children's
Books, an Hachette UK company.

www.hachette.co.uk

Contents

Inauguration

On a clear and sunny January morning in 2009, the biggest crowd in the history of Washington DC – around 1.8 million people – gathered in front of the US **Capitol Building**. They had come to watch the **inauguration** of Barack Hussein Obama as the 44th President of the United States.

In a colourful ceremony that was watched by millions all over the world, the audience was treated to a mixture of music, prayers, speeches and poems. The 'Queen of Soul' Aretha Franklin sang *My Country, 'Tis of Thee.*

In his 19-minute inaugural address, Barack promised to attend to the serious problems facing America. He constantly referred

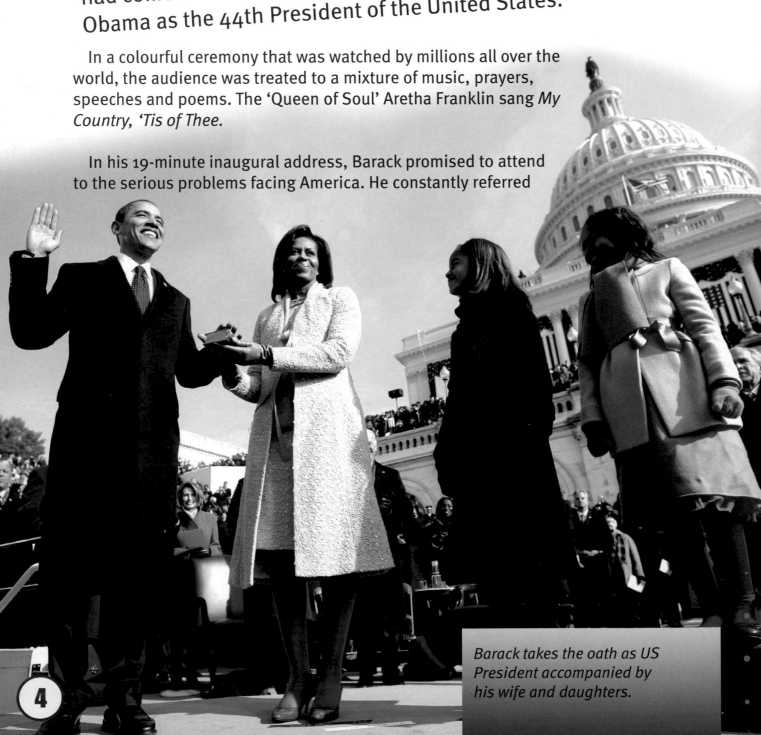

Barack takes the oath as US President accompanied by his wife and daughters.

to previous generations who had made sacrifices in the cause of America. He sent a message to the world, saying: "... know that America is a friend of each nation and every man, woman and child who seeks a future of peace and dignity."

After a luncheon, the Obama family watched the two-hour inaugural parade. In the evening, Barack and his wife Michelle danced at ten inaugural balls! Their first dance was accompanied by Beyoncé singing the song *At Last*. America had sworn in its first African-American President.

WOW!

All new presidents of the US have to swear an oath of office on the Bible. Amazingly, Chief Justice John Roberts read out part of the oath incorrectly! To make sure everything was legal, the oath was re-taken the next evening.

A huge crowd flocked to the National Mall in Washington DC to watch the inauguration.

Barack's Family

Barack Obama was born on 4 August, 1961 in Honolulu, Hawaii, USA, the son of Ann Durham and Barack Obama Senior (Snr). His parents had met at the University of Hawaii in a Russian language class! They fell in love and married on 2 February, 1961. Ann was only 18 and Barack Snr, an exchange student from Nyanza Province in Kenya, was 23. Sadly, the marriage did not last. When Barack was two years old, his father won a scholarship to Harvard University, but could not afford to take his family. The couple separated and divorced in 1964.

Barack's mother Ann had a huge influence on her son. She was very bright, able and deeply knowledgeable about philosophy and foreign cultures. She was a very kind person who saw the good in people. This impressed Barack who noted, "it was how she operated" and he "saw the good effect it had on other people."

Ann's parents, Barack's grandparents, Stanley and Madelyn remember her as a single-minded daughter who did not care what other people thought.

Barack Obama Snr was a gifted student and became a chief economist in Kenya.

WOW!

Barack's mother was actually christened 'Stanley Ann Durham' – her father wanted a son! She was teased mercilessly when young as 'Stanley Steamer' or 'Stan the Man'.

When Ann's parents moved to Texas, Ann made friends with a black girl. This was not popular and Ann suffered abuse from others because of this.

After her divorce from Barack Snr, Ann married Lolo Soetoro, a foreign student from Indonesia. In 1967, the government ordered that all Indonesian students abroad had to return home. Lolo returned first, followed by Ann and Barack.

INSPIRATION

The young Barack with his mother, Ann. She was an important influence on him.

"I know that she was the kindest, most generous spirit I have ever known, and that what is best in me I owe to her." Barack about his mother.

Life in Indonesia

When 'Barry' (as Barack was called in his youth) was six years old a Pan Am jet took him and his mother to a new life in Jakarta, Indonesia. Lolo was waiting for them at the airport and they drove to their new home on the outskirts of the city.

Barack in Indonesia with his mother, step-father and half-sister, Maya. Sadly, Lolo died of liver disease in 1987.

WOW!

While he lived in Indonesia, Barry experienced a very exotic diet! This is a description of what he ate: "Small green chilli peppers raw ... dog meat (tough), snake meat (tougher) and roasted grasshopper (crunchy)!"

Barack's step-father Lolo saw to it that Barry stood up for himself. After a fight with another boy over a stolen football, Lolo brought home some boxing gloves and taught Barack how to box and defend himself.

Barry was a very quick learner and picked up the Indonesian language and customs in less than six months. He was shocked at the poverty he saw around him and Lolo insisted he could not give money to every beggar who came to the door. Importantly, Barry witnessed the harshness of life. One year the local farmers suffered terrible drought; the next year it rained for a month and he saw livestock and homes swept away.

The Soetoro family house in Jakarta, Indonesia.

During this time Ann and Lolo had a child, Maya, Barry's half-sister. Gradually Barry's mother worried that his education was suffering and she supplemented his schooling with an American **correspondence course**. Ann taught him from 4 am before he went to school.

When Barry complained he was tired, Ann snapped back, "This is no picnic for me either!" After a nasty accident when Barry gashed his arm badly on a barbed wire fence while mud-sliding, Ann made the decision that he would do better returning to Hawaii.

school and college

In 1971 at the age of ten, Barry returned to Hawaii to live with his grandparents. Ann and Maya joined him in 1972. His grandparents had helped him enrol at an exclusive Preparatory School, Panahou Academy.

Barack with his maternal grandparents, Stanley and Madelyn Dunham. They had a major impact on him.

Barry found settling in to Panahou difficult. Most pupils came from wealthy families and his class was 90 per cent white so he felt like an outsider. There was only one other black pupil in his class – a girl called Coretta. One day they were playing together and the other boys shouted, "Coretta has a boyfriend!" Barry, deeply embarrassed, pushed her away, shouting, "Leave me alone!" Ever since then he has regretted his betrayal.

During Christmas 1971, Barry's father came to visit the family in Hawaii. It was the only time Barack Snr properly met his son. There were arguments between them when Barack Snr criticised Barry for watching too much television and neglecting his school work. During this time, Barack Snr talked to Barry's class about Kenya, which was a great success.

INSPIRATION

Barack Obama about his time in Hawaii: "The opportunity that Hawaii offered – to experience a variety of cultures in a climate of mutual respect – became ... a basis for the values I hold most dear."

The Low Memorial Library at Columbia University in New York.

TOP TIP

Barack Obama Snr, who tragically died in a car accident in 1982, once said: "Confidence – the secret to a man's success."

As he got older, Barry became obsessed with basketball. He felt at ease playing basketball and practised every day. He was part of the highly successful school team but was mainly used as a substitute.

In 1979, Barry graduated from Panahou and went to university at Occidental College, in Los Angeles. It was here that Barack (as he now preferred to be called) discovered that he had a talent for public speaking. At a rally protesting against apartheid in South Africa, he enjoyed the feeling of having people listen to him.

In 1981, Barack transferred to Columbia University in New York and graduated in 1983 with a BA in political science. What was he going to do with his life?

The world of work

Barack's first job was at Business International Corporation when he was 22. It was a company that helped American firms that traded abroad. He did not particularly enjoy the job, but it taught him a lot about the world of business and international trade. He left after a year, determined to do something to help people and, as he told his grandmother, "to leave the world a better place."

In 1985, he applied to become a community organizer in a very poor district in Chicago's South Side – Roseland and West Pullman. On a low salary of $13,000 (approximately £8,000 a year), Barack's job was to make a difference to the lives of the mainly black residents who were directly affected by poverty, crime, poor housing, unemployment and a growing drug problem.

Barack visiting his paternal grandmother, Sarah Obama, in Kenya in 2006.

INSPIRATION

Barack attended the Trinity United Church in Chicago and heard its pastor Jeremiah Wright give a sermon entitled 'the **audacity** of hope.' Barack became a devout Christian.

In the three years Barack was in Chicago's South Side, he worked closely with the many Christian churches and achieved a number of successes. Altgeld Gardens was a huge run-down apartment complex in a badly-polluted part of the city. Barack helped the inhabitants force the local authority to remove the very dangerous **asbestos** from their homes. Other successes included introducing a neighbourhood Employment and Training Centre and a tutoring and counselling programme in local schools to help prevent at-risk teenagers turning to crime.

Barack was becoming frustrated, because he needed to understand the legal system if he was going to improve people's lives and that meant getting a law degree. He applied to the best law school in America – Harvard – and was accepted! Before he started, Barack decided to travel.

He toured Europe before travelling to Kenya to meet his father's family. He stayed with his half-sister, Auma and the time he spent with the family helped Barack understand a little more about who he was.

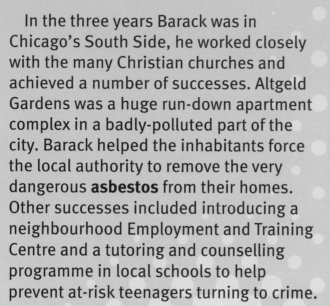

HONOURS BOARD

Barack's favourite musicians:
Miles Davis
John Coltrane
Bob Dylan
Stevie Wonder
J. S. Bach

Barack met his cousin, Pasqual in Kenya in the late 1980s.

Law school success

The 27-year-old Barack who began studying at Harvard Law School in the autumn of 1988 was not a typical Harvard undergraduate. He had worked for four years, three of which were in the tough South Side of Chicago; he had travelled in Europe and Africa. Because of these experiences, Barack was very mature and incredibly self-disciplined and he threw himself whole-heartedly into his law studies.

TOP TIP

When Barack graduated from Harvard with a Juris Doctor (professional doctorate in law), it was awarded with 'magna cum laude,' Latin for 'with great praise' and one of the highest levels of degree.

Barack wrote many articles for the Harvard Civil Rights-Civil Liberties Law Review.

Although Barack made friends with lots of students on the **campus**, he spent a good deal of time on his own, especially in Harvard's poorly lit libraries. He had to study and learn important cases and trials in American legal history and understand the laws or 'statutes.' Barack felt very strongly that Harvard students were privileged and that after they gained their law degrees they should do all they could to help people who were less fortunate than them.

Barack experienced great success as a writer for the *Harvard Law Review,* a highly respected legal journal that was written by some of the school's most able students. By the end of his first year he had been selected as an editor of the *Review*. In his second year, friends tried to persuade him to stand for president of the *Review*, but Barack told them he wasn't interested. At the very last minute he decided to stand and joined a field of 19 editors all trying to become the president.

After a long election, in which candidates were eliminated one by one, Barack was triumphant, becoming the first African-American president in the *Review's* long history! This success was recognised by the national **media** and *The New York Times* ran a profile on the young up-and-coming lawyer! He was getting noticed.

The Harvard Law Review *class photo (1991). Barack, as president of the* Review, *is sitting in the centre.*

A day in the life of President Obama

The alarm rings at 6.30 am and Barack Obama, the 44th American President, gets out of bed to face another day as the world's most powerful man.

He tries to see his two daughters, Malia and Natasha (Sasha), in the morning – they might share breakfast – but he definitely sees them off to school. Barack then does a short work-out in the White House gym and then work starts.

INSPIRATION

"Let us unite in banishing fear ... we cannot fail." President F. D. Roosevelt in his first radio 'fireside chat' broadcast in March 1933. Barack is a great admirer of Roosevelt.

The President is helped by his Personal Secretary, Katie Johnson.

A meeting about the economy was broadcast live on the White House website.

The President spends the first 45 minutes of his work day reading important national security **briefings** and then he skim reads four or five daily newspapers to learn how his new policies are being received. His Personal Secretary, Katie Johnson hands him the letters to sign. Every day, ten letters are chosen from the mountain of mail the President receives and he reads them the night before. They are personally answered and he feels it is a very good way of keeping in touch with the problems of ordinary Americans.

The President then starts a series of meetings with his senior staff, including Joe Biden his vice-president and Robert Gibbs his Press Secretary, in which he is briefed on important issues of the day. One committee might discuss hurricane awareness, while another might address tobacco advertising aimed at children. Lunch is usually taken during these meetings, the so-called 'working lunch'. On 2 June 2009 Barack drove to the nearby Five Guys burger bar to buy lunch for his staff. He caused a sensation when he walked in and ordered ten burgers! Barack chose a cheeseburger with fries.

On one day of the week, the President records his weekly Internet address, which can be watched on the White House website. He finishes work about 6.30 pm and the next two hours are exclusively for his family. They have dinner together, hang out with Bo, the family dog, and then the girls go to bed about 8.30 pm.

The President admits he is a night-owl and works and reads until about 12.30 am or later before going to sleep.

17

Lawyer, husband, teacher and writer

When Barack studied at Harvard he did a holiday job at the respected Chicago law firm Sidley Austin in the summer of 1989. He was **mentored** by a highly successful lawyer called Michelle Robinson. Barack was immediately smitten, but Michelle was more reserved and resisted his requests for a date. She finally agreed and they began dating. Barack returned to Harvard, but their long-distance relationship survived and in 1991 they became engaged. On 3 October 1992 they were married by the Reverend Jeremiah Wright at the Trinity United Church in Chicago.

HONOURS BOARD

Barack has written three books:

Dreams from My Father (1995)
The Audacity of Hope (2006)
Change We Can Believe In (2008)

This is a wedding photo of Barack and Michelle Obama.

Barack graduated from Harvard in 1991. Before practising law, he became director of the Illinois Project Vote which aimed to get as many as possible of the 400,000 unregistered African-Americans registered to vote for the November 1992 Presidential election. It was very successful and registered 150,000 voters and this helped win Illinois for the Democrat, Bill Clinton who then became President.

After the election, Barack joined the Chicago law firm of Miner, Burnhill and Galland. It was the perfect placement, for they specialised in contesting injustices through legal actions in the courts. Barack never actually conducted trials, but worked as a team lawyer preparing cases. And as if he was not busy enough, he also became a professor of constitutional law at the University of Chicago between 1992 and 2004.

Incredibly, while Barack was working on the Project Vote during the day, he was working late into the night on his book *Dreams from*

My Father – a Story of Race and Inheritance, which was published in 1995. This work routine put pressure on the newly-married couple, because Michelle liked going to bed early and getting up at 4.30 am!

WOW!

"Barack didn't pledge riches, only a life that would be interesting. On that promise he's delivered." Michelle Obama talking about Barack's wedding vows.

Bill Clinton and his wife, Hillary celebrate his victory in the 1992 election.

The Senate

At the age of 34, Barack entered politics and in 1996 he was elected to the state **Senate**, the local government for the State of Illinois. Barack stood for the 13th District, an area that included Chicago's South Side, and won an easy victory for the Democratic Party against the Republican Party. In 2000, Barack failed to get nominated as the Democratic candidate when he ran for the **House of Representatives** in Washington DC.

Barack announced his candidacy for the US Senate in 2003. In 2004, with 53 per cent of the vote, he gained the Democratic Party **nomination**. Barack made the **keynote speech** at the Democratic National Convention and spoke of unity: "There's not a black America and a white America and a Latino and Asian America, there's the United States of America ... We are one people."

Barack and Michelle Obama during Barack's campaign to be elected to the US Senate.

Senator Obama stands with his family as he is sworn into Senate by US Vice-President, Dick Cheney.

After an exhausting campaign against his rival Republican candidate, Barack won the election to the Senate by 70 per cent to 29 per cent. This was the largest margin of victory the state of Illinois had ever seen. Meanwhile, the Republican George Bush had been elected as President of the United States.

Barack was only the fifth African-American Senator in US history and the third to be popularly elected. Senator Obama became very popular in Washington and sponsored laws ranging from making the workings of government more open, to relief for the Republic of Congo in Africa.

Barack had enjoyed a **meteoric** rise in the world of politics and people began to ask if he would stand for President in 2008.

TOP TIP

Barack uses as much social media as possible including podcasts, Twitter, MySpace, Facebook and YouTube. You can follow him on Twitter or email the White House.

The Democratic nomination

Throughout 2005 and 2006, Barack had been busy writing his second book, *The Audacity of Hope: Thoughts on Reclaiming the American Dream*. The book outlines his beliefs, how he adopted them and his ideas on family life, religion and race. Writing it was not easy, for as well as being a Senator and parent, he had spent a year writing late into the night and he was exhausted.

Hillary Clinton was a strong opponent in the contest for Democratic nomination.

In the summer of 2006, the family took a trip to Africa that would include visits to South Africa, Ethiopia, Chad, Djibouti and Kenya. The trip was a success, although huge adoring crowds caused the family problems. Because of the crush, a two-hour trip to visit his grandmother in Kenya only lasted half an hour.

More and more people were asking if Barack would stand for the Presidency. After much thought, soul searching and close discussions between Barack and Michelle, on 10 February 2007, he announced his candidacy for President in 2008!

Barack was joined by seven other candidates all trying to win the nomination for the Democratic Party. However, his main opponent was the very able Hillary Clinton, wife of the former President, Bill Clinton. The contest was very close, some states supporting Barack, others backing Hillary.

INSPIRATION

"Michelle was a mainstay during big moments in the campaign, comforting him when necessary and firing him up when necessary."

Barack wins the support of the state of South Carolina.

In February 2008 a group of musicians led by will.i.am put the 'Yes We Can' speech to music. It's had over 19 million hits on YouTube!

After a defeat in New Hampshire, Barack made an inspiring speech. He said that when in America's history there had been difficulties, Americans had "responded with a simple **creed** that sums up the spirit of a people: Yes We Can ... Yes we can to justice and equality ... Yes we can heal this nation. Yes we can repair the world."

On 7 June, Hillary conceded defeat and Barack was chosen as the 2008 Presidential candidate.

The 2008 Presidential election

Barack's opponent in the election was the 72-year-old Republican Senator for Arizona, John McCain. Campaigning started in September for the election on 3 November. Both came from outside mainland America – Barack from Hawaii and John from the Panama Canal Zone.

The main issues that dominated the campaign were the poor condition of the **economy**, the Iraq war, healthcare and terrorism. Both candidates were able to argue these points in three Presidential debates held in September and October. It was estimated that the first one held on 26 September attracted 52.4 million viewers. According to CNN polls after the debates, Barack won all three.

TOP TIP

Work with people who are better than you. Barack chose Joe Biden, a more experienced politician than himself. He knows the Presidency is too big for one man and will need sound advice.

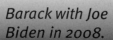
Barack with Joe Biden in 2008.

Barack chose as his Vice-Presidential **running mate** experienced Delaware Senator Joe Biden. John McCain's choice caused great excitement when he chose his, the **governor** of Alaska, Sarah Palin. Never in American history had a woman stood for such high office.

During October the Obama family received very sad news. Barack's grandmother Madelyn, to whom he owed so much, was dying of cancer. On 23 October, Barack suspended his campaign for two days so he could be with Madelyn who was gravely ill. He had always regretted not being able to be with his mother Ann, when she too died of cancer in 1995. Sadly, Madelyn died on 2 November 2008.

INSPIRATION

"She has really been the rock of the family, the foundation of the family. Whatever strength, discipline that I have, it was from her." Barack Obama, talking about his grandmother on 23 October 2008.

When the votes were counted, it was found that 52.9 per cent had gone to Barack and 45.7 per cent to John McCain. Obama became the 44th President of the United States and is the first-ever African-American to hold this office.

Barack waves to the crowd in Chicago after winning the election.

The 2012 Presidential election

On 7 November 2012, Barack Obama won the 2012 Presidential election. By winning his second term in office, Barack joined FD Roosevelt, Dwight Eisenhower and Ronald Reagan as the only presidents of the last century to win more than 50 per cent of the popular vote.

INSPIRATION

"And I wouldn't be the man I am today without the woman who agreed to marry me 20 years ago. Let me say this publicly. Michelle, I have never loved you more. I have never been prouder to watch the rest of America fall in love with you too as our nation's first lady."

Barack talks about his wife in his victory speech on 7 November 2012.

Romney and Obama debate issues on the campaign trail in October 2012.

Mitt Romney's running mate was Paul Ryan, a US Congressman serving Wisconsin's 1st District. Barack Obama chose vice president John Biden to be his running mate for the second time.

The two candidates took part in political debates and ran energetic campaigns across the country. The main issues that dominated the campaign were the struggling economy in light of the worldwide **recession**, taxes and foreign policy. The political debates between the presidential candidates had tens of millions of television viewers. Mitt Romney was successful in the first of the three campaign debates and he gained support over issues to do with the economy.

In late October 2012, the northeastern parts of the USA were hit by a ferocious storm known as Hurricane Sandy. The damage caused in New York was particularly severe. Barack, in the middle of his campaign trail, claimed that responding to the situation was his "first priority." He left his campaign to survey the storm damage. His response added to his popular support and took the attention away from Mitt Romney's discussions about the economy and taxes. Barack also importantly managed to keep hold of his support bases from the last election, which covered a wide range of different groups. The US public seemed to prefer Barack's less conservative views on social issues.

When the votes were counted Barack came out on top with 50.6 per cent of the votes with Mitt Romney getting 47.8 per cent. Barack Obama secured his re-election as the first African-American President.

Obama gives his victory speech on 7 November 2012 and thanks his family and his running mate.

The impact of Barack Obama

In some ways the election of Barack Obama shows how much America has changed. In 1961, the year of his birth, many of the southern states were still **segregated** and parts of many places – restaurants, bars, theatres, hotels, buses and bus stations – were out of bounds to black Americans. Even parts of the capital, Washington DC, were off-limits to African embassy officials. Barack Obama has said: "I don't look like other Presidents on the dollar bill!"

President Obama meets troops at Camp Victory in Baghdad, Iraq in April 2009.

That an African-American family has made it to the White House is testament to the courageous work of the civil rights movement of the 1950s and 1960s. The inspirational leadership of Martin Luther King – tragically assassinated in 1968 – is echoed in a lot of Barack's words and actions.

Expectations of Barack's Presidency were and are extremely high. He has had great achievements during his time in office. Barack has put in place major healthcare reforms. His main aim is to make healthcare more affordable and to cover up to 50 million Americans who don't have medical **insurance**.

In 2009 Barack was awarded the Nobel Peace Prize for his diplomacy and efforts to strengthen relationships between nations. Barack has tried to improve relations internationally while remaining determined to protect the USA from threats of terrorism. In 2011, Barack announced the end to the Iraq war as had been promised and US troops returned home by the end of that year.

Barack has injected funds into the economy, firstly in 2009, and then in 2012 he promised to inject a further $ 200 billion. His aim has been to create jobs and revive manufacturing but Barack's critics have claimed that he should be more concerned with lowering American debt. The struggling US economy has been Barack's biggest challenge to date and this issue led to many people backing Mitt Romney in the last election. In 2008 Barack was the candidate for change. He has had some great successes during his time in office and many American people still believe he can deliver the change he promised.

INSPIRATION

The Constitution of the United States of America inspires President Obama:
"WE THE PEOPLE of the United States, in order to form a more perfect union... "

Many challenges face Obama in the attempt to make America a 'more perfect union'.

Have you got what it takes to be a politician? Try this!

1) Do you believe that the world could be a better place?
a) Yes, definitely – there are so many challenges facing the world.
b) Yes, but there's nothing we can do.
c) No, things are OK as they are.

2) Are you interested in world and current affairs?
a) Yes, I always watch the news and read a newspaper.
b) I sometimes watch the news but not regularly.
c) No, I find them boring.

3) Would you be happy to speak or take part in a school assembly?
a) Yes, I am quite a confident public speaker.
b) I answer and speak in class, but I'm not confident in front of an audience.
c) No, I am a bit shy when speaking in front of people.

4) Are you involved in your school's Student Council?
a) Yes, it's a good way of improving conditions at school.
b) I know about it, but I'm not really involved.
c) I don't really take much notice of it.

5) If you wanted to improve facilities for young people in your area, what would you do?
a) Write a letter to the local newspaper and get in touch with the local councillor.
b) Moan about it to my friends!
c) I'm not sure.

6) How do you react when people verbally criticise you?
a) I listen to their arguments, but I'm quite thick-skinned so it doesn't bother me.
b) I try and stick up for myself, but I don't like it.
c) I get quite upset when I get criticised.

RESULTS

Mostly As: You seem to have a number of qualities that a politician needs! When you get older you might want to join a political party and get involved locally at first.

Mostly Bs: You show interest in some aspects of politics, but you need to find a cause or campaign that really fires you up!

Mostly Cs: You don't really seem cut out for politics! Perhaps when you get older you will see how politics affects everyone's lives.

Glossary

apartheid   A system that used to exist in South Africa that separated people of different race or colour.

asbestos   A material that protects and insulates from fire and heat. Exposure to it can damage the lungs.

audacity   A strong type of courage or confidence.

BA   Abbreviation for a Bachelor of Arts degree. This is the degree that Barack graduated from Columbia University with.

briefings   Sets of important information on particular topics.

campus   The buildings and land of a university or college.

Capitol Building   This is the meeting place of the United States Congress. It is in Washington, on top of Capitol Hill.

civil rights   The rights and freedoms that everyone has in society irrespective of race, colour or belief.

correspondence course   A course of study that is conducted by post.

creed   A person's beliefs.

economy   The system of trade and industry from which a country gets its wealth.

governor   The elected person in charge of an individual state in the USA.

House of Representatives   The lower house of the American Congress.

inauguration   When someone takes up an official position with a special ceremony.

insurance   A system where people pay money in advance to cover the costs if theft, damage or ill-health occurs in their lives.

keynote speech   The most important speech in a conference or meeting.

media   The way that information is spread in society, through newspapers, television, radio or the Internet.

mentored   This is when someone, who is usually more experienced, helps and advises someone else.

meteoric   A rapid or sudden advancement.

nomination   When someone is officially chosen to do a particular job.

recession   When a country's economy stops growing.

running mate   In the US elections, the person the presidential candidate chooses to be their future Vice President.

segregated   When people are kept separate or apart because of their colour or race.

Senate   The upper house of the American Congress.

Index